"THE ARMOR OF GOD"
EPHESIANS 6:10—18

BY
Adriana Carrera

Original title:
GOD'S MIGHTY WARRIOR

Text:
Adriana Carrera

Illustration and Layout:
Niurka Alba

Style correction:
Carolina Manzo

Impression:
ADP Printing & Signs

Copyright© All Rights Reserved. Published by:
Four Winds Community Church
info@fourwindscom.org
10303 Royal Palm Blvd, Coral Springs Fl 33065
Phone 954-825-8272

First Edition 2023
ISBN: 979-8-859-03169-6

Printed in the United States of America

GOD'S MIGHTY WARRIOR

"THE ARMOR OF GOD"
EPHESIANS 6:10—18

BY
Adriana Carrera

Finally, be strong in the Lord and in his mighty power. Put on the full armor of God, so that you can take your stand against the devil's schemes. For our struggle is not against flesh and blood, but against the rulers, against the authorities, against the powers of this dark world and against the spiritual forces of evil in the heavenly realms. Therefore, put on the full armor of God, so that when the day of evil comes, you may be able to stand your ground, and after you have done everything, to stand. Stand firm then, with the belt of truth buckled around your waist, with the breastplate of righteousness in place, and with your feet fitted with the readiness that comes from the gospel of peace. In addition to all this, take up the shield of faith, with which you can extinguish all the flaming arrows of the evil one. Take the helmet of salvation and the sword of the Spirit, which is the word of God.

Daniel and Sophia love God and they go to church every Sunday.

One day, Carolina, their Sunday School teacher, taught them about the Armor of God that is in Ephesians 6:10-18

"I didn't know that we are at war!" Said Daniel.

"Yes Daniel, but this is an invisible war against our enemy, the devil."

Carolina answered.

"This is the Armor of God!" Said Carolina showing them the graphic.

THE ARMOR OF GOD:

BELT OF TRUTH
Satan fights with lies. If you wear it, it will protect you from being deceived.

BREASTPLATE OF RIGHTEOUSNESS

The enemy attacks your heart and emotions, but you are forgiven and accepted by faith.

THE SHOES OF THE GOSPEL OF PEACE

Be ready and available to give Jesus' love to others and spread the Good News.

THE HELMET OF SALVATION

Protects your mind. The enemy wants us to doubt God. Jesus is our Salvation

SHIELD OF FAITH

Protects you from being hurt by insults and temptations.

THE SWORD OF THE SPIRIT

Trust in the truth of the Bible, which is the Word of God.

The Good news is that Jesus already
won this battle on the cross
where He paid for all our sins.

He conquered death because He resurrected
on the third day and defeated the devil.

"Then why do we have to wear this armor?"
Sophia asked.

"Because we live in a fallen world.
It's important to be warriors
until the Lord comes
for the second time around!"

Their teacher explained.

Yesterday I was playing
and broke a vase." Paul said.

"Did you tell your mom?"
Rebecca asked.

"Nooo! She forbids me
to play inside the house
with the ball.
I hid all the pieces."
Paul answered.

"Our teacher at church
said that we need to be
always truthful."
Sophia explains.

"My teacher said that we fight an invisible war between Good and Evil." Sophia tells Paul.

"She taught us to wear the belt of truth, which is the Bible! The commandments say, 'Do Not Lie'"
"But I haven't lied!" Paul exclaims.

"Until she finds out!" Sophia replies.
"Is this war like the superheroes?" Rebecca asks.
"Yes, but there is just one superhero, Jesus! We are His soldiers" Sophia answers.

"Paul, if you are one of His soldiers, be brave and confess to your mom. Tell her you are sorry and you will never do that again." Sophia says to Paul.

"If you talk to your friends about Jesus' love for all His children, you are wearing the Shoes of the Gospel of Peace." Carolina says to the kids.

"I did that just yesterday with my friends Paul and Rebecca!" Said Sophia raising her hand.

"The Shield of Faith is to believe without any doubt that God is always with you when you are sad or having a problem." Carolina says.

"A kid at my school told me I have big ears. They all laughed at me." Daniel says with sadness.

"Daniel, we will always encounter someone that is going to make fun of us, but what is important is what you think about yourself. Those jokes are like arrows to hurt your heart. If we wear the armor, those arrows are not going to get in." Carolina explains to him.

"Jesus told us in John 10:10 that the devil came to steal, kill, and destroy, but Jesus came to give us a plentiful life.
What's more important? What the kid said or what God thinks about you?"
The teacher asked.

"But what does God think of me?"
Daniel asks.

"He thinks of you as His prince! You are chosen and He loves you so much.
What your classmate did was wrong but you must forgive him." She says.

Our teacher told us that we need to fight an invisible war, but a very real enemy, wearing the Armor of God. It's not a uniform! It is believing in Jesus and the Bible.

That is the Armor!

Made in United States
Troutdale, OR
11/25/2024

25344650R00017